Mrs. Tightwad's Guide to Buying a Car

Naomi L McCreadie, AKA Mrs. Tightwad

Dedication

For my sweet husband, Thomas, who cheered on my every effort and supported me each day I sat to type like a mad woman. Thank you for being my Mr. Tightwad.

Alannah – my precious baby girl…thank you for keeping on me when I really didn't feel like writing. You kept me moving forward.

Helen – my adorable oldest baby girl…thank you for wanting to learn more and keeping me laughing when I got too stressed and forgot to myself.

Bryant Thomas – For being Grammy's sweet little guy.

Mark Wiskeman – Thank you for your input and your editorial skills. Your eye as a sales manager along with your skills for details are definitely appreciated.

Table of Contents

Chapter 10 – Buying a Car With Derogatory Credit

Prologue

These days, the stress of our daily lives can take its toll. We become ill-tempered and rarely do we have time to even think about ourselves and the relaxation we so desperately deserve. This can only be compounded when our ever faithful vehicles start to show their age and begin to nickel and dime us to death, or their high mileage teeters on the brink of being historic.

It is important to note that I see more people than not that walk into the dealership with a complete and total "I'm going to be a jerk and get what I want" attitude. Granted, you're there to buy a car and get the best price possible. However, if you want to act like a jerk and treat the people you expect to help you like they are nothing more than trained monkeys, then perhaps you need a serious dose of reality. To treat someone in such a way that you can see them begin to shake out of anger as their face turns some unique shade of crimson, congratulations.....you are a bully and may get your butt tossed out of the showroom before you even get a chance to begin negotiating.

I know you want to save money otherwise, you wouldn't have bought this book. However, understand that if you do bully your way into a deal, don't expect the salesperson to go out of their way to help you when you need something like the shuttle service (if the dealership offers it), or to be accommodating and make sure they take all the time needed to ensure you are familiar with all of the features of your new car. If you make the salesperson uncomfortable during the sales process, they are in no way required to continue working with you.

Instead, understand that each dealership has specific protocol that the salespeople must follow. Most salespeople will take a genuine interest in you, what you do, your family, etc. They can, over time, become trusted and valuable friends. Behave in such a way that if you were that salesperson, you would want to work with that person and do everything in your power to assist them. It's ok to want to reach a particular goal, as long as you treat the person who is working 70 hours a week and barely gets time with their family with some respect. Do this, and you can come away a winner and with your integrity intact.

Furthermore, the majority of books I have seen out there on this very same topic tell you hold the dealership accountable for all of the discounts. The only problem with this concept is that the discount is only one small part of the whole savings concept. The majority of the savings has got to come from you otherwise you will still end up spending money you really didn't need to.

As you go through this book, understand that it is written from a standpoint of being completely straight to the point. You can't expect everyone to give you the savings....you need to bring something to the table as well. Follow the advice contained within the next 10 chapters and you will be fine.

Chapter 1 – Setting The Budget

If you already have a car payment, then this should be easy for you. Just keep in mind that if you have been in your current vehicle for just a couple of years and you have a 72 month term, you will most likely have negative equity that will get carried over to the new loan and can increase your payment. It's important to understand this and be prepared for it.

There are so many factors that come in to play when you are buying a car, it can be quite scary and very intimidating. The easiest thing to do is to look at your monthly budget and figure out what you can spend each month. And I cannot stress this enough.....UNLESS YOU ARE PAYING FOR THE VEHICLE IN FULL WITH

CASH, DON'T FOCUS ON THE BOTTOM LINE!! People budget by the month, not by the full purchase price, so don't get caught up in what the final total is.

Another thing you need to take into consideration is your take home pay. While banks look at what you gross monthly or annually, you need to look at your net. If after all of your bills and expenses you have a whole $200 left, you are not going to be able to afford to buy a new car (unless you are putting the majority of the price down in cash), let alone a used one. When you figure the cost of insurance as well as operating expenses, you will see the total cost of ownership far exceeds that $200.

So let's say you have a monthly take home pay of $3200. Rent is $750, electric is $120, $100 for cable, $300 for food, $125 for water and sewerage, and $50 for rubbish removal.

That means you have $1445 in monthly expenses. That also means you have $1775 left over. That does not mean that it is all disposable. You want to bank at least 50% of that for emergencies. In other words, you can afford $800 a month in car and insurance payments. NOTE: I do not recommend spending that amount if it can be avoided. By not taking on that huge of a payment, you will be able to keep paying on your car fairly easily should your income change for the worse.

When you set your budget for your car, this is when you need to be both realistic and wise. Just because you can afford the $60,000 car doesn't mean that you need it, or should buy it. It's all about choosing what is right for your situation and knowing when to curb yourself. Too many times people have run out and purchased the $90k Escalade only to realize that not only was it not practical for them, it also was not a smart purchase. This brings me to my next point........

PRACTICALITY

Everyone's situation is different, and what you need may be very, very different from what you *think* you need. Most salespeople are experts at getting to the very heart of what a customer's needs are. Sometimes they fall in line with what the customer came in on; other times, not so much.

The practical nature of your car purchase is going to boil down to several things: number of people in the household, distance traveled to work, whether or not a vehicle has been financed in the past, credit rating (more on this later), type of work, hobbies, vacationing habits, where you live, and whether or not this will be a primary or secondary vehicle.

Ok, so let's say that you have two children, and a spouse. You all love to travel by car on vacation. You have another vehicle, a compact 4-cylinder sedan, driven by your spouse back and forth to their job 15 miles a day one way. You live in the northern part of the U.S and your kids are big into sports. Your commute to work is about 25 miles one way. What do you choose?

A) A mid-sized sedan; i.e. - Malibu or the Altima

B) A compact sedan; i.e. - Prius or Accent

C)Full-sized SUV; i.e. - Vera Cruz or Pathfinder

D)Small Crossover; i.e. - SRX or Rogue

For this scenario, the small crossover may be the ideal option since most often come with 4 cylinder engines and have great fuel economy, they are available in all wheel drive (AWD), have ample cargo space, and are far more affordable than their larger counterparts.

So you can see that the salesperson's job can be quite complex. Their ultimate goal, while yes it is to sell you a car, it is also to make sure you are happy with your purchase. Why? Because if you are pleased with the way the salesperson did their job, you are more likely to return a few years later and purchase from them again and refer friends and family to see them.

Think about it......if you were treated badly and felt as though you were forced to buy a certain vehicle because the salesperson didn't ask you barely any questions and really didn't listen to your concerns, would you buy from them again? Highly unlikely. And I know what you are thinking....."I wouldn't buy from them in the first place!" Believe it or not, a large number of extremely intelligent people do just that. We will get into that a little deeper later on.

True Story

A man and his wife walk in to the dealership one day with a clear picture of what they wanted....the full-on platinum edition of the Armada. It was a gorgeous vehicle, complete with a gorgeous MSRP to match of $55,000.00. With the posted price of $43,000.00, this vehicle was a steal. At least it would be for the right buyer. In doing the needs assessment, I discovered that their income and their credit scores would not allow for this kind of payment, one that was close to my housing payment. It took more than 45 minutes for it to sink in that what they *wanted wasn't what they needed. They only had two children, and with both of them making moderate incomes of about $35k a year each, it just was not a good fit.*

Ultimately, we stepped down to the much smaller Rogue with all of the bells and whistles, a vehicle that still suited all of their needs and still fell within their budget. Because they allowed me to do my job the way I needed to, they ended up being very happy people and have a vehicle that they can easily afford.

Chapter 2 – Choosing The Right Vehicle

So many times people become extremely overwhelmed with the number of choices that they have when it comes to vehicles, they often confuse themselves badly. There are ways to avoid this and the answer may be no further away than your closest dealership. The first thing you need to do is decide which class of vehicle you are looking to purchase. Buying the wrong type of vehicle can lead to loads of problems down the road, one of them being negative equity when you go to trade and get into the right vehicle. This will cost you thousands of dollars and will lead to higher payments if you don't have a down payment set aside to offset the negative equity.

Buying the wrong vehicle is easier than you think. We get distracted by all these incredible features we see advertised on TV that we think to ourselves, "That is just what I need." Before we know it, we are at the dealership, buying the vehicle without ever having really asked ourselves, "is this what I *really* need?"

Here's the common classes of vehicles. This list with descriptions and examples will help narrow things down for you and make your car purchase easier.

Sub-Compact – The smallest of the sedans, often found in a hatchback form as well. Have excellent fuel economy, have 4-cylinder engines, and can get 40 mpg or better on the highway. This is an economy class vehicle, so there may be fewer options available. Low in price and can generally be found with either the automatic or manual transmission. Cars in this class include Prius, Sonic, Accent, Versa, and Versa Note.

Compact - The next size up of sedans. Still with the 4 cylinder engine with a little bit more displacement. Torque and horsepower in this class is better than in the subcompact. Most manufacturers' models have ample trunk space and can be purchased with just the entry level options or the fully loaded set of options. Manual transmissions may be difficult to find in this class, since the automatic transmissions tend to get better gas mileage. Cars in this class include Sentra, Elantra, Cruze, and Corolla.

Mid-Sized – In general, the most popular size class of sedan available. Most often found with a 4 cylinder engine, although 6 cylinder may be available. Gas mileage can be around 38 mpg on the highway. This class gives buyers the opportunity to buy a car that, when fully loaded, can be like a luxury vehicle without the luxury price. Cars in this class inlcude the Altima, Sonata, Camry, Mazda 6.

Coupe – This class of car is strictly a two-door and is idolized by the sports car enthusiast. Not a practical choice for a family vehicle, since access to the back seat can be difficult. Most manufacturers offer both FWD and RWD coupes of different types and sizes. Convertibles also fall into this class more often than not, although there have been manufacturers that have produced convertibles in unconventional vehicles where one would not expect to see that feature. These care are known for their flashy looks and their speed. RWD models do poorly in the winter, so take that into consideration if you live in a snowy climate. Cars in this class include the Corvette, Mustang, and GTR.

Full-Sized – This class is generally comprised of 6 or 8 cylinder engine sedans. There are also more luxury sedans in this class than any other class. Cars in this class include the Maxima and the Cadillac CTS.

Small Crossover – This class of vehicle takes the best parts of a sedan and combines them with the best parts of an SUV. Typically 4 cylinder in nature, they are generally available in both Front Wheel Drive (FWD) as well as All Wheel Drive (AWD). AWD models get a little bit less gas mileage than the FWD models, but both are spacious and can be purchased with basic amenities, or the full-on, fully-loaded, all the bells and whistles style. Vehicles in this class include the Rogue and the Tucson.

Mid-Sized Crossover – Aside from being larger, the only difference between this class and it's smaller counterpart is the size of the engine. Some manufacturers offer trim level that will make the vehicle a complete luxury vehicle. Examples of this class are the Murano and the Lexus GX 460.

Compact SUV – This class of vehicle is designed for the people who live life just as much off-road as they do on. With the flexibility to go from one extreme to another, this is a great choice for the people who love adventures. It is available in different trim levels, automatic, manual, 4X4, or just a Rear Wheel Drive (RWD). Vehicles in this class include the Jeep Wrangler.

Full-Size SUV – Unlike its smaller cousin, the full-size SUV is designed for larger families and often is seen with 3rd row seating. It is spacious and it's flexibility allows for ample cargo space when needed. Trim levels go from basic to fully-loaded and offer amenities that can suit the tastes and needs of everyone who is shopping for this type of vehicle. Primarily seen as a 4X4, RWD models also do exist and they also are available with factory-installed towing packages. Some manufacturers are now offering Hybrid models of this type of SUV. Gas mileage is generally lower than that of the Crossovers. Vehicles in this class include the Explorer, Pathfinder, and Suburban.

Small Pickup – These days regular cab trucks are a tough find. More often than not you will see the extended cab or the crew cab, a 4 door version of the pickup designed for families. These vehicle are ideal for the people who want the ability to tow or haul as demand requires it. Usually found with either a 4 cylinder or 6 cylinder engine, these trucks are made for very light duty. Manual transmissions are available as is 4X4, however, finding a 4X4 in a 4 cylinder engine is extremely difficult as the added weight combined with the fact that towing with these trucks can easily destroy the engine and is not recommended. Trucks in this class include the Ranger and the S10.

Full-Size Pickup – The trucks are meant to be heavy duty. Some manufacturers offer two-three different sub-classes of these vehicles depending on the customer's needs. Like their smaller counterpart, these trucks are also generally no longer found in a regular cab, come in both 4X4 and RWD varieties, and have the choice of transmissions. They come in 6 cylinder and 8 cylinder varieties and often have the heavy duty towing package factory installed. These are great options for the person who works in construction, or who needs to haul a lot of tools and ladders. Farm owners also enjoy this truck. These trucks can be fitted with a fifth-wheel hitch to be able to attach a goose neck trailer. General sizes can include the ½ –

ton, ¾ – ton, and 1 ton and trucks in this class include the F150, F250, Ram, Silverado, and Titan.

Mini Vans – No longer a vehicle strictly for the soccer moms, the mini van has evolved into a versatile family vehicle. This class combines ample cargo space, AWD/4X4 availability, easy access to all doors and seat rows, with today's style and functionality. Some manufacturers have 3rd row seating available in their models and a towing package may come already factory installed for the family that has a small camper to tow. There are often two different sizes available. Vehicles in this class include the Odyssey, Voyager, and Quest.

So by now, you have a good understanding as to what's out there and what it's purpose is. The next chapter will teach you how your credit will affect your car buying decision, important things you need to know to get financed, and when it is time to be realistic about your expectations.

Opting For Certified Pre-Owned/Used

Savings can be had just by simply switching your focus from a new vehicle to a certified pre-owned. Most CPO vehicles have a better warranty on them than on a new vehicle, and this being the case, that makes it a much better choice for you. They have to meet very stringent requirements put in place by the manufacturers, so these cars, depending on manufacturer, can have a limited warranty that exceeds a new car warranty. More often than not, again, depending on the brand, a potential CPO car cannot have more than one owner, cannot have more than 60k miles, cannot have any accidents on its history, and must pass approximately 165 points during the certification inspection. If the car cannot meet the primary requirements, then it cannot be certified.

Any dealership that you want to deal with should be able to provide you the CarFax on the particular vehicle(s) you are interested in. If it has a clean CarFax, is a clean vehicle and was well maintained, and has relatively low miles for its age, then keep that as a viable option. Pre-owned vehicles can help you save a lot of money, and may be just the ticket when it comes to keeping payments to a minimum.

Doing Your Due Diligence

I can remember back in the day when shopping for a vehicle was so much different than it is today. Dealerships didn't have computers at their disposal to print up paperwork, and taking delivery of your new vehicle often happened three days after the paperwork was completed. Sales managers used the actual Kelley Blue Book to put a value to a trade, which could be a lengthy process, and the internet hadn't even become an idea yet.

Today, you have a wealth of information at your fingertips.....so use it. Do the research on the particular models that interest you and narrow it down to just three. I say this simply because if you don't do this, not only are you going to waste an enormous amount of time test-driving every single model, but you will also confused the dickens out of yourself, and wind up making the process more stressful than what it needs to be. After three vehicles whether in one day or on separate days, the features and characteristics of each start to blend together, making it impossible to differentiate one from another. But more on test drives here in a little bit.

There is a serious reason as to why I say to narrow it down to three….remember a time when you went into a candle shop and began sniffing everything in sight. After about the third candle, every other candle had hints of what the previous ones did, correct? Your nose retains particles of the fragrances you just smelled and becomes confused until you clear the air, so to speak. Your brain is no different. After three vehicles, your brain will retain small pieces of each one, at which point, your brain becomes confused and can't sort which piece goes to what vehicle. This is why it is vitally important to narrow down your choices otherwise you could end up buying a vehicle that you ultimately hate.

When you are narrowing things down, you need to decide what is more important to you. Is it the gas mileage, or is it the safety features? Maybe it has more to do with a particular brand or size. Perhaps you are more feature oriented and are looking for the best bang for your buck. Whatever the case may be, this is an area that needs proper attention before you start actually going to the dealerships. Keep in mind that what you want may be a whole lot different than what you THINK you want. To get an idea as to how often this affects people, take a look at dealership's used inventory online and see how many nearly new vehicles there are listed with mileage under 15k. These are vehicles that were traded by people who bought what they thought they wanted or needed only to find out that they were wrong on some level. This can cost a person thousands of dollars. But don't stress; there is an easy way to prevent that from happening.

Getting Ready To Hit The Dealerships

Now that you have your options limited down to three, it's time to select the dealership(s). What you are looking for are the specific vehicles you are interested in, and this is where color choices come in to play. But it is also where price comes in to play. For whatever brands you are interested in, look for the dealerships that are going to give you the greatest discount. Posted price dealerships (ones that post their prices online below invoice and do not negotiate) are the best option. Since they do not negotiate on the vehicle price, don't ask....you'll be wasting time. The other upside to this is that this format of dealership was designed to take the stress out of buying a car. If they offer a maintenance package that gives you routine maintenance for "free" for the lifetime of your vehicle, consider it. Just like in couponing, it's better to spend a fraction up front to save thousands of dollars in the long run.

Another type of dealership out there is the negotiable posted price dealership. This one operates like a posted price, but may be willing to negotiate the price a little bit. If they offer services for free, compare the savings of this to the posted price dealership and see which one will save you the most money.

Be wary of the dealership that, when you show up on the lot and say you saw a certain car online, will tell you that their internet price is different than their lot price. The lot price is generally higher than the internet price and is meant to make negotiating a bit more difficult, particularly if you love the car. Using this tactic, dealerships have made a lot of money because the consumer hasn't been diligent enough to know that they can dictate how this goes forward by simply saying, "You can't test drive a car online and you can't deliver a car online. See ya!" Either the dealership will want to work with you or they won't. If they don't, don't sweat it. Once you have clearly stated that you saw a car online, that makes you an internet customer and you are entitled to the internet price.

Yet another type of dealership is the traditional dealership. These are the ones who will start off at MSRP and negotiate until the break of dawn and the roosters are crowing. They will do everything they can to hold every penny possible. Sure, you will get the rebates you are entitled to, but be warned…this negotiation process with them can take several hours of your life and your time is valuable and has a dollar value. It's time you will never get back once it is gone, so why waste it?

More often than not, traditional dealerships will have addendum stickers on the windows of the vehicles right beside the Monroni sticker. These add-ons are usually for things such as edge guards for on the doors, pin striping, and other upgrades that could ultimately add as much as $2,000.00 to a car's sticker price. If you don't want those items, speak up before you even sit down at the desk with the salesperson. Make it known completely that you don't want it, plain and simple. Don't let them try to sell you on why you need it.

Bear in mind, distance will also play a part. If you are planning on driving 3 hours just because a dealership has the best price on the internet, be smart and weigh that against the amount of time you will spend traveling, at the dealership, and add in the cost of fuel. You could actually end up spending more in the long run when you figure all of this together.

Now that you are ready to hit the lot, make sure you print out the page of the car you are interested in driving and pop in to the dealership. Scheduling an appointment to take a test drive is preferred and ensures that there will be ample time to focus on you and answer all of your questions. If you cannot make the appointment, have the courtesy to call the dealership and let them know so you can reschedule. It's only polite and it's what you would hope people would do for you, correct? Pulling a no-call-no-show for an appointment is very poor form and will not get you taken seriously as a buyer. Of course, there are the emergencies that do pop up unexpectedly, however, the percentage of those are actually extremely small, while the rate of no-shows is rather high in comparison.

Not knowing what you really need can be an enormously costly mistake on your part, so be prepared to let the salesperson do their job and get the facts of what it is you really need and see if your needs and wants match up. If they do, it's a winner. If they don't, try the salesperson's recommendation and see how it fits. Salespeople are masters at ferreting out the facts, so the harder this process becomes, that is on you. The more you resist, the more of your valuable time you are wasting, and whether or not you realize it, your time has a dollar value so don't waste it. I think I just said that, didn't I?

Make sure that you bring a notepad with you, and have it divided into two columns. One column should read "Likes", while the other reads "Dislikes". Do this for all three cars you test drive and make sure the name of each model is at the top of each page so you can keep yourself straight. Once you are done with the test drive, make your notes of your likes and dislikes in the appropriate columns and add any additional notes at the bottom. You'll also want to make note of the price the dealership is asking for as well and any freebies you may get as a buyer. After all of the test driving is done and the notes are completed, if the dislikes outweigh the likes, cross that car off of the list and move on to the next vehicle. If the opposite is true and the likes column is greater, then keep that car on the list of choices as a viable option. The car with the greatest amount of advantages is the clear choice for you.

Using this technique to find the right car is only helpful if you are completely honest with yourself and remain unbiased so that you won't unconsciously sway your decision one way or the other. This is when you need to stay clear-headed and focused so you can get to the goal.....ownership.

Now that you have found your perfect vehicle, it is time to work on the negotiations. And even though you may be dealing with a posted price dealership, there are still some negotiations you can do. Let's move forward and see what can be negotiable, and when.

Chapter 3 – Negotiating The Price

Negotiating is where most people get really tied up in knots. It is the primary reason why people get so stressed when they go to a dealership. When it comes right down to it, you really just want the best possible price that you can get. There is nothing wrong with that. The biggest thing you need to keep in mind when dealing with a dealership is to not act like a complete donkey's hind end when negotiating. Remember, the dealership is under no legal obligation to do business with you and if you become belligerent, verbally abusive, or otherwise cause a scene, you could be asked to leave and told to never return. Negotiations require tact. Those aforementioned actions show a lack of class and tact, and actually makes the person look like a bully.

The first thing you need to do before you even started negotiating is to remember the type of dealership you are at. If you are at a posted price dealership, do not even think for a second you are going to be able to get even more of a discount. If you have done your research, you will have known by this point that the vehicles are priced below invoice. Where you can negotiate is on any additional products or services, as well as the interest rate (in most cases). Generally speaking, where posted price dealerships are concerned, do not expect them to give up the whole thing and give you everything at their cost.....not going to happen. Dealerships need to be able to pay their bills, too. If everyone wanted everything at the dealership's cost, the business would not be able to sustain that kind of loss and would end up eventually closing their doors. As for a bit of a discount, you would do yourself an injustice if you didn't at least shoot for one.

True Story

On a particularly quiet day, a man comes in with his girlfriend and her daughter. The man was interested in a new truck with plenty of bells and whistles, but still had the ability to tow and haul light loads. We found the truck of his dreams in a beautiful shade of gray.

During the negotiation process, the daughter became extremely rude and was practically yelling at the top of her lungs as to what she wanted for her mom's boyfriend. Mind you, this girl was not paying for the vehicle, nor was she going to be on the title. The mother, sat there embarrassed, and my blood pressure hit the roof. Since he was paying cash and the daughter was acting like a complete fool, I was infuriated that someone would have the audacity to speak like that and make a complete spectacle.

When I went to my sales manager, I didn't need to say a word. He could clearly hear everything she said. My ears were burning red and I was shaking out of anger. All I wanted was to just tell them to have a nice day and tell the daughter to not EVER come back.

After nearly an hour of the abuse and me begging my manager to just let me bid them farewell, the daughter succumbed to the price. She politely asked if we could throw in a set of wind deflectors and a bug deflector, installed. Since she became polite, we agreed.

Before they left, the daughter clearly stated that she was a little crazy and hadn't taken her meds. My response? I told her that I appreciated that fact and asked her nicely to not ever come back unless she was stable. Her mother smiled and apologized for her adult daughter's bad behavior. The man thanked me for my time and patience (if he only knew!).

All I can say is....unless you want to be a complete spectacle, don't behave like that. You won't get what you are looking for that way, unless you think that creating a scene will help you out. That whole scene could have resulted much worse than what it did.

Oddly enough, other patrons praised me for not blowing my top and knocking someone's lights out.

Paying Cash vs. Financing

The biggest thing you need to keep in the forefront of your mind is how you are going to pay for the car; either you will be paying for it up front fully, or you will be financing. If you choose to pay for the vehicle fully and up front, remember that you very likely will be giving up a rebate, which could cost you in the long run. Some of these rebates amount to $1000 or more. The better option for you is to finance for the short term. That is to say, since there are no prepayment penalties, there is also no law that says that you are required to keep the loan for the full term. In other words, pay off the loan in three to four months after signing the papers. This way you keep the rebate in place AND you have a paid a minute fraction of what the total interest would have been on the full term.

When you do finance for the short term, you can put down as much as you'd like, as long as you are financing the banks minimum amount. It is suggested that you don't put down more than 50%. By doing this, you are not using all of your liquid assets, and should a crisis arise (and we all know that the unexpected can happen at any possible moment turning your life upside down), you still have a low monthly payment to fall back on should you need to extend past your original plans.

When you finance for the long term, NEVER focus your negotiations on the total On The Road (OTR) price. You should always be focused on the payment, since that is how you budget your money. Part of this will come in to play with the interest rate that you qualify for, and may or may not be negotiable. If it is, and you are able to take that rate down a point or two, you will be working to save extra money each month off of your payment. You can argue bottom line all you want, but if you don't qualify for a prime interest rate, then you may not be able to get the payment you are looking for. This, of course, goes to credit score which we will talk about in the next chapter.

Whatever course of action you decide to take, keep your focus on the end result…..that new car that you are about to become the proud owner of.

Chapter 4 – Understanding Your Credit

This is the chapter where I get real and tell it like it is. The first area you will learn to save money on a vehicle is in the financing, and it's all about the interest rate. I have this early on in the book simply because you need to understand that if you have marginal credit, you may not be getting that payment you want on the car you want. Too many times I have seen people who have bad credit walk onto the lot with all the attitude they can muster only to snap at a salesperson and say that they want to buy the $53,000.00 car with no money down. This is a red flag for salespeople, since easy sales like this are very few and far between.

In reality, you should be monitoring your credit, and if you're not, shame on you. You should always know where your credit score is and why it is there. The reason for this is simple....the lower your credit score, the higher of an interest rate you will have, the more you will end up paying out in interest, and the more difficult it is to get financed. The higher the credit score, the more prime interest rates and programs you can qualify for. Credit score also determines whether or not a bank will finance you and if you will be REQUIRED to put money down.

Don't get me wrong, the past few years has hit a lot of people hard and the economy has hurt some people who were genuinely interested in maintaining a good credit profile. However, there are those out there that, one look at their complete file will tell you the truth....they don't pay any of their bills. I recently met a woman who between her and her husband, had more than $100k a year in income. She handled legal documents for a bank and he was an attorney. Her credit was so bad that she couldn't get financed by a second-chance lender.

Banks are not going to lend money to just anyone. They look at the ability to repay the loan, past credit experiences, whether or not there has been anything sent to collections, bankruptcies, judgments, and the overall file. That is not to say that someone who has had a bankruptcy that was discharged can't get financed, because they can. They are just more difficult to place. We will cover certain obstacles and buying a car with derogatory credit in another chapter.

Here are a few key phrases that you may hear/see:

Ghost – You have no credit file and therefore have no score. It's tougher to get financed by a conventional bank with this issue, but it can be done. Sometimes a co-signer is required, as may be a down payment. You will probably end up with a higher interest rate.

Thin file – Your credit is limited. Your score may be good, but if you have never had a loan for more than $10k, or you have had only one or two revolving accounts, this can lead to a higher interest rate. Like the ghost, a down payment or a qualified co-signer may be needed.

Qualified co – This is a person who is willing to co-sign for you and has at least a 720 credit score and a low debt to income ratio.

Bullet – These people are a salespersons dream and is where you want to be. Bullets easily qualify for all the special incentives including $0 down and 0% interest. These people have a credit score of 780 or higher.

Debt To Income Ratio – The percentage of debt in direct relationship to the total amount of income. This is figured as a formula: Income/debt=percentage

The Reality

This book is about saving money when buying a car, but I do have to be very straightforward here. I am not the type of person to sugar coat anything and tell people what they want to hear. I tell people what they need to hear. Sometimes you may not like it, you may not even agree with it. But I am not about lying to people to sell a book, a car, or anything else for that matter. That having been said.....this is where I get seriously real.

If you have a credit score of 425 and no money down, you are not going to be able to buy that $53,000 Armada. It just is not going to happen. Even if you were to be approved, it is not a smart decision money-wise since your interest rate would be through the roof, as would your payments. This is how many people get into financial trouble to begin with. By financing the majority, if not all, of a high ticket vehicle, they are committing a very large portion of their income to the payment. Then when a crisis hits, they are unable to make these payments, which leads to repossession, and that leads to a bad credit file. That is where you don't want to be.

Saving money when buying a car starts with the selling price and ends with the interest rate. When you're dealing with a low credit score, it is important to remember the more money you can put down, the better off you will be. This is for several reasons; 1) that means less interest you will be paying over the life of the loan, 2) you will be more attractive to a bank and may be able to get a slightly lower rate, and, 3) your payments overall will be lower.

Having a 425 credit score doesn't make you a bad person. Perhaps you have absolutely no credit aside from a couple of minor things that may have had a negative impact. Or perhaps you at one time were a bullet and you ended up losing your job because of the economy the way thousands across this county have. Regardless, you need to build/rebuild your credit, and a good way to do that is with a car payment that is roughly 30% of your disposable income.

True Story

It never ceases to amaze me as to how many people really don't have an idea as to what their credit is, or even how it works. Proof positive of this comes walking into the dealership on a daily basis. One day this was in the form of a young lady who was in need of a vehicle that would be economical for her job where she had a 30 minute commute one way.

I showed her a couple of options and after a test drive, she decided that the Versa Sedan she was interested in was an ideal fit.

While her income was more than sufficient, she wanted to buy with no money down. A quick credit app would reveal that she was going to have to lay out some cash.

Her credit score was in the mid 500's and while there was a low-limit credit card and some derogatory medical bills, we were still able to secure an approval for her with the bank requiring $2,000.00 down. This is usually where my work REALLY begins.

I had to have a discussion with her about the whole approval and what it was going to take on her part to be able to buy the car. This also meant a higher interest rate and ultimately a higher payment. It was a tough pill for her to swallow, but in reality, she had no idea that her credit score was low and that the $200 a month payment she wanted was out of her realm of possibilities. More so, she didn't even realize until I educated her that derogatory medical bills have a negative impact on the credit score.

In the end, her father, who lived three states away, loaned her the down payment and we were able to get her on her way, happy as can be.

Bear in mind, not all stories end up being happy ones and that the average person has no clue about their credit.

Let's say that after all of your bills, you have $1,000 left over at the end of the month. Then feasibly you should be able to afford a maximum payment of $300 per month. If you already have a car payment and are planning on trading that vehicle in, then figure in that payment you already make as part of your disposable income (DI) as though you don't have a payment at all. In other words, your current car payment is $300 and your disposable income is $1000. That makes your DI $1300 and your max payment $390. This helps to absorb any negative equity you may have.

Not All Credit Scores Are Created Equal

It doesn't matter in the grand scheme of things as to how high your credit score is…what matters is how high your score is AND how your credit profile looks to the banks. In a nutshell, you can have two people, both with 720 credit scores. One will be approved at a prime rate of 1.9% while the other will be approved at a rate of 5.9%. That's a huge difference, correct?

The problem here isn't the dealership, so for those of you who have had a situation like this and got the slightly higher interest rate, don't fly off the handle and blow up at the salesperson or the sales managers. The problem is solely yours and the key is in your credit profile. Let me explain.

The 720 with the low interest rate will have the great mix of credit, maybe have a credit card or two and also have perhaps a mortgage and/or another car loan. There is a mix of the different types of credit, although the length of the loans may be a bit on the shorter side and the payment history, while there, may not be fully appreciated.

The 720 with the slightly higher interest rate may only have student loans and a credit card or two, and that's it to the credit profile. This leaves for very little information for the banks to base their decision on since there is no history of having had a large loan that had been maintained well.

While this information in a sense may seem to go against how the credit score is computed in the first place, in reality, this is an anomaly and can be seen fairly often. This is why it is imperative that while you are building credit, you keep a good mix of the types of credit. Once again, I highly advise those that are trying to build a good solid credit profile to consult with a credit counselor and get professional advisement.

If You Don't Use It, You Lose It

It is completely true what they say….if you don't use it, you lose it. This is because as time goes on, old credit files, depending on what they are, will drop off of your credit profile. If you are paying for everything in full at the time of purchase, you are not "updating" your credit to maintain or raise your score. One can, over the course of several years, once again become a ghost and have to start from scratch all over again, thus costing yourself thousands in high interest payments.

I can understand wanting to pay cash for everything. After all, it's no fun having a ton of debt hanging over your head. However, the wiser choice is to finance for the short term. Only put down what you have to even if you have all of the cash available. I know I sound like a broken record, but many a person has been stuck in bad situations after laying out thousands on a car only to be smacked right between the eyes with a major crisis and not have the liquid assets to be there during that emergency.

When you lay out a large amount of money for the down payment, you are far better off taking a term for 48 to 60 months, even if you intend on paying off the loan within just a couple of months. This gives you some wiggle room, and of course, if you suddenly find yourself in a predicament, you have the minimum monthly payment to fall back on.

An important thing to remember is that with financing for the short term, you want to keep the payments for at the very least 3 months. The reason behind this is very simple: most states do not process title work quickly. This gives the new title time to catch up. And by allowing time for the title to catch up, you are also ensuring that you won't lose any valuable rebates you were able to take advantage of. Losing those rebates even after the fact will cost you money, a realization that is not too pleasant to find out about when you pay off the loan. In a nutshell, don't be hasty.

How Credit Is Computed

The way credit scores are figured has been a mystery for the average consumer since the inception of the system. It is a complex algorithm that defines your ability and likelihood to repay any type of loan. When banks look at your credit score, they can see as to how creditworthy you really are in just a glance. Roughly 25% of the U.S. population has a credit score that is above 780. Given the number of people in the country, that is a remarkably small percentage. Of course the average person makes every effort to take care of their bills and obligations. However, there are those in the population who don't give their debts a second thought, and those are the ones that prime banks want to stay away from.

More than two decades ago, Fair Isaac Corp. developed a complex formula for calculating a person's credit score. To this day, the FICO score is one that is most well-known and most often used. Their formula is still proprietary. What is not well known is that there are specific parts of your credit that are weighted, or given a higher consideration than others, depending on the importance of the information. How you pay your bills is weighted at 35%, while other areas, such as the mix of credit types is weighted at 10%.

Credit scores range from 300 (worst) to 850 (best). Even though most lenders will use the FICO score, they will sometimes run the person's information through their own system and formula. Some dealerships may do this and come up with a BEACON score which may be a little bit lower than the FICO score. The BEACON looks at the credit score in the worst case scenario....if the client did not pay the next month's bills. This method is typically only used for those with marginal credit and helps the dealership locate the best options for financing.

If you haven't been monitoring your credit, you need to be, especially if you are trying to rebuild or establish yourself. Knowing where your credit score is at any given moment in time is vitally important for you and can help prevent thousands of dollars lost as a result of identity theft. Using and online resource such as creditkarma.com or freecreditreport.com can assist you in monitoring. They also have tools that can show you what your credit score would do in different scenarios. This is something that each person should understand before they try to take on any additional loans or payments.

No matter where your credit score is, that is the one thing that will determine your finance rate. Ironically, it is also used in determining your insurance premiums. While your cost for insurance is largely made up of your credit score, there are other factors that go in to computing that such as driving history, DUI's, length of time with the previous insurance company, age, and lapses in policies. I'm not going to go into insurance in depth here since it can be so complex, but I feel that it's important to understand.

Getting back to how your credit score will affect your car payments, another thing that is EXTREMELY important to remember is that when you are out shopping for a vehicle, especially if you are credit challenged, do not let your credit be run until you have decided on a vehicle. Some dealerships will shotgun your credit application to every single bank they work with. All of those hits are call inquiries and they can send red flags to lenders if there are a lot of them. They also can impair your credit and inquiries stay on your credit profile for up to two years.

The whole idea of the credit score, as you can see, can be very complex. In keeping it simple, the higher the score, the better off you are, and the less you will spend on interest.

Purchase Vs Lease

Despite what you have learned throughout your entire life, just because you finance a vehicle doesn't mean you own it. You are in the process of buying it....for however long that term may be for. Even if you have financed for 72 months, have made 70 payments and stop there, the bank will repossess your car, end of story. It sounds crazy, I know. You would be surprised at the number of people who miscalculate their payments and end up in that very situation.

Some states are a two-part title state, meaning that when you finance the vehicle, you are sent one part of the title that contains all of the information including the lienholder. Once the final payment has been made, then the bank will send you the other part of the title, thus releasing you from the lien. Until that point, you cannot do anything with the vehicle with the exception of trading it in to a dealership. The idea of owning the vehicle until it is completely paid off is a fallacy.

This is where leasing becomes a smarter option for those that aren't paying cash for the car, and it is far more flexible, particularly for those with excellent to outstanding credit.

Gone are the days of having to over stress about the number of miles you have driven in a year. While the industry standard in 15,000 miles per year, a slight overage will not hurt unless you are going to turn in the vehicle and walk away from the brand altogether. Instead, you can, as in a traditional ownership, trade in the vehicle towards your next lease. Or if you really love the car, finance the residual balance on the short term, that is, for three or four years.

The best parts about a lease is that you always know up front when you go into the finance office as to how much your vehicle will be worth at the end of the term. There's no guessing game about it. On top of that, you can have a payment that is quite often less than that of a financed 72 month term. Since you're really only paying for the portion of the car that you're using during the lease term, this makes for an ideal arrangement if you like to trade every couple of years to get into the newest technology.

But the biggest benefit to a lease is that you will never, EVER have to deal with negative equity. Why? It is because at the end of the term of the lease, your payments are done. When you go to make that last payment, you can decide as to what you want to do; buy out the vehicle and finance the balance, trade into a new vehicle lease, or turn it in altogether and step into a new brand. It is with this last choice that mileage becomes a concern.

There are also more perks for leases. Some manufacturers may offer a lease loyalty program, which gives more discounts than a traditional loan would. Regardless of the lease program, a 15k mile a year lease should be the highest mileage limit you have. To prepay for higher mileage is not a good idea and will cost you a chunk of money. Instead, refer to the other options that will benefit you greater without costing you a serious wad of cash, such as financing/buying out the residual balance. No matter what, the biggest thing you need to remember is that unless you have a credit score of 740 or higher, leasing may not be a good option since clients are judged on tiers. Tier1 gets all of the good benefits, while the lower in tier you go, the higher the money factor will be and the more will be required up front. The money factor is a type of interest rate, and just like all interest rates, is completely affected by your credit score.

So, to sum it all up, credit score determines a lot when it comes to buying a car. The better your credit score, the more money you will save. We will touch more on bad credit situations and how you can still buy a car and save money later one. For now, let's start talking about everyone's least favorite topic….the down payment.

Chapter 5 – Coming Up With The Down

Once again, I'm going to get realistic here….this part of the purchase process is one that most people try to avoid. Simply put, most people either don't want to or cannot come up with a down payment. Some figure that it's a good way to save money. Well, I'm going to put it straight to you. Unless you have perfect credit and can get approved for 0% interest on the loan with payments you can afford, then you better add this phrase to your vocabulary: DOWN PAYMENT.

The logic behind the down is very simple. Even with a decent credit score in the mid 600's will mean a higher interest rate. If you get approved with $0 down and have a $500 trade, you are doing yourself a serious injustice. You will be spending thousands of dollars on interest and will undoubtedly want to go to a 72 month term to have the most affordable payment possible. Here's a piece of advice…..come up with a down payment! Don't be a chucklehead and expect the dealership to give in to your whim just because you think you should not have to pony up the cash. Newsflash….it's your responsibility, it will be your car, it will be your loan. It takes two to make the deal work and if you're not willing to be realistic about what you are trying to accomplish, then perhaps you need to buy a bicycle and use that for your sole mode of transportation. I know it sounds harsh, but all too many people walk onto the car lot who have less than perfect credit scores and insist that they can get that $300 a month payment on that $40,000.00 car with $0 down.

I know what you are thinking…."How exactly am I saving money if I'm putting down money on a car?" The answer is very simple. The less you finance, the less you will pay in finance charges, especially if you have less than perfect credit. The lower the credit score, the higher your interest rate will be. The more money you put down, the less you will spend overall.

Bear in mind that some banks will have a minimum that you can finance and that usually varies between $7,000.00 to $10,000.00 depending on the bank. Even more, if you are trying to build or rebuild your credit, you need to be financing at least

$10,000.00 for it to have the most positive impact possible on your credit score.

Don't Be Negative

Another nice thing about the down payment is that aside from keeping the payment lower, it will also keep the negative equity lower as well. Some banks, when they calculate the interest, don't have an "early payoff scale". This basically means that regardless of how quickly you pay off the vehicle, the same amount of interest will accrue. This can pose a serious problem if you are wanting to trade into a newer model vehicle and you had financed the full purchase price without any down payment whatsoever.

Negative equity is something that most people don't even take into consideration until it is far too late. Since it is typically caused by a multitude of factors coming together all into one not-so-harmonious situation, most people find out in the long run that they should have put some money down and went for the vehicle that had some amenities in it, rather than the base model.

The harsh reality is that what the vehicle is worth at the time of trade in and what you owe on the vehicle are two entirely different things and one has NOTHING to do with the other. It is not the dealership's responsibility to get you out of that loan. You're the one who signed the original contract, it is your debt, you agreed to the terms.

When you roll that negative equity into the new vehicle, you are, in essence, financing a chunk of the old vehicle all over again. Since you are not going to own that car anymore, that is a total waste of your hard-earned money.

As much as the average person would love to buy a new car with $0 down, the reality is that you shouldn't avoid the down payment. This is particularly true if you can't afford it. This is where I have to spit out another truth....if you are looking at a $50,000.00 vehicle, it is not the responsibility of the dealership to get you to that $400 a month payment. You have a whole lot of responsibility here, and you need to own it.

A good rule of thumb, fairly true of the average buyer with decent credit, you can expect about $20 a month in payment for every $1,000.00 financed. So let's say that a gorgeous $37,000.00 vehicle has you completely head over heels in love with it. Your ballpark payment would be somewhere in the vicinity of about $740/mo. With excellent credit, you can reasonably expect to be somewhere around $555/mo. By using these formulas, the above can help you find a vehicle that will fit your budget.

The biggest rule of finding the right car to fit your budget.....face the reality that what you want may not be what you can afford.

Chapter 6 – Putting A Value To Your Trade

Nothing frustrates a car buyer more than walking into a dealership with a preconceived notion of what their trade vehicle is worth. In all seriousness, you need to do a little research beforehand, but understand that what you think your car is worth may be completely wrong.

Case in point - I have seen people literally walk into a dealership wanting to trade a 2003 Ford Contour that had a serious accident to the tune of $10,000.00 on the CarFax and had 169,000 miles on the odometer, had dents, dings, and rust, and they expected $5,000.00 for it. Let's face it, most people have some kind of attachment to their vehicles, and that's ok. What is not ok is to tell people who deal with this kind of situation day in and day out that you know better than they do as to what the vehicle is worth. Do yourself a favor and take a good hard look at your car with a very critical eye and write down all of the flaws that you would fix this very moment if you had the means to. This does not mean to go over the top and picture your car tricked out with underglow and graphics. It means to look at the car in such a way as to look at the flaws that you would repair to get it to as pristine a condition as possible given its age, mileage, etc.

Getting To The Facts

It is a fact that a car that has had more than two owners, it has a lower value. It is a fact that a car that has had a catastrophic accident will see a lower value than one that has not. It is a fact that how the average person views the condition of a vehicle is a matter of opinion and *not* a matter of fact.

Again, be realistic. Make a list of the flaws on the outside and the inside of the vehicle and make sure you write down the complete VIN number as well as the actual current mileage. You will also want to have the date handy of the most recent service you have had that cost more than $200, the total amount of any insurance claims, the condition of the tires, and have an idea as to whether or not all of the service records are available. There is a reason why I am telling you to gather all of this information, and it's not for Kelley Blue Book.

KBB is a good resource, but there are caveats. One of them is that the values are not regionalized. They are very general, and what I mean by that is that the value of any given vehicle in one part of the U.S. is nearly the same as that of another. In other words, the value of a 4X4 pickup truck is close to being the same, regardless of the part of the country you are in. In reality, a 4X4 truck will have a greater value in the northern part of the country than it generally does in Hawaii, Arizona, Mississippi, and so on.

Another issue is that KBB does not ask for specifics. It does not ask you to put in any damages that there are on or in the vehicle. This is problematic because once you get to the end, you are asked to select your vehicle's condition, such as Poor, Fair, Good, etc. This is where the matter of opinion comes in to play, and that eliminates the matter of fact.

A better resource to use that will give you both a retail value and a Buy Guarantee is AutoTrader.com's Trade In Marketplace. This tool makes you get specific on the damages and it eliminates the opinions. Since business and finance is based on fact, this keeps the value true to life and relevant for your area. You may not like what the tool tells you for a value, but at least you have the truth.

The TIM tool will prompt you through a page of basic questions, then a page of specific questions, including any equipment that may have been added as an aftermarket item. The two final questions on this page you will want to answer no to, since most people are not mechanics. Even though I work in the auto industry, I still have no idea as to whether or not a particular car or truck has a twisted frame unless it is abundantly apparent.

The following page will allow you to review all of your input and choices you have made. If there is something you need to correct, you will have the opportunity to edit the information should you forget something pertinent. Once you click on submit button, it's generally a matter of just a few seconds before you get your vehicle's value. Occasionally, you will land on a page that implies that the site needs a harder look at your vehicle. What this really means is that a pair of human eyes is looking at your car's information in order to come up with a very real dollar value. This is a good thing.

True Story

One day a customer and his daughter comes in to the dealership and is looking at a Sentra. They have a 10-year-old Ford Contour to trade that has no tread left on the tires, multiple scratches on the paint, stained carpeting that is beyond repair, 250k miles and a CarFax that showed a major accident years ago with an insurance claim of about $10,000.00.

I ran their trade through the TIM tool and the vehicle value came up at a whole $150. That is not a typo. The father was so absurdly offended by this value that he wouldn't even allow me to have my manager look at the *trade to see if we could put a higher value on it. He even went so far as to accuse me of manipulating the computer program in such a way that I was able to falsify the information, even though he sat there beside me as I put all the information in and ok'd it before submission.*

The sad reality was that he had so much sentimental value wrapped up in that car, that he was blinded by the truth of its real worth in the marketplace. After all, the car had seen two proms, a wedding day, and the birth of a grandchild.

Once in a while I get surprised by the TIM tool and I see a vehicle value that is higher than what I would have expected. The key here is to remember that as much as you may love your car or truck, it will always have more value to you than it does in the real world.

Once you get the value certificate printed out, you have three days to take that in to a dealership. The good part about this is that as long as you have been completely honest with your answers, you will have a buy-back guarantee on your trade. This means that if the dealerships offer you less than what you have as a value, AutoTrader will buy your car from you. Let's see KBB do that!!

I have a lot of fun with people who think that the car they rolled up in with the dents in the fender and the mud-caked interior. (Yes, that has happened.) My favorite words to hear are "I saw ABC Cars had this same vehicle for sale for $9500.00 with the same kind of mileage." A quick hit on the TIM tool tells me that the car is worth $4000.00 with its bald tires, scratched paint and stained carpeting and seats.

Now, think seriously about this for a second, because I know either you have or someone you know has done this. In the above situation, I tell the person what we need to do to the car before it is put out on to the lot and the cost, which is generally about $1500 if it doesn't need tires. Of course, we need to try and make a profit on it, so I tell them that we are going to add about $2000 to that to make the asking price $13,000 if we were to give them the $9500 they were asking for. That's when I ask very bluntly if they would pay $13,000.00 for their car. They obviously answer no in such a way that the next state over can hear their response. No one in their right mind would.

Think about this carefully….if you want retail price for your vehicle, sell it privately. You WILL NOT get retail value for your trade from a dealership, so don't waste your valuable time asking for it. Remember this cardinal rule: your time is valuable and has a dollar value (I will probably say that a couple of more times throughout this book). The more time you waste trying to fight battles you will not win, the worse off you are. Unless the dealership is completely busy and the finance office is totally tied up, buying a car should take you no more than 2 hours from the time you walk in until the time you leave with your new car. (Difficult to place loans may take longer.)

Another thing to keep in mind is that all those dents and dings that are on your car will lower the value. Too many times I see people who value their trade on KBB and come in with this air of arrogance and bluntly state that their trade is valued at $6,000.00. One look at their 10-year-old car to understand that they view their vehicle as being in excellent condition, when in reality the body damage tells a different story.

True Story

A customer comes on to the lot with his parents one day looking for a Sentra. The parents were the ones buying the car and their trade was certainly an interesting vehicle. Their car was about 8 years old, had only roughly 60,000 miles on it, and as I was doing my walk-around, the son proudly stated that they valued the car on KBB and it was worth $12,000.00.

As I walked around to the passenger side of the car, I looked up at the son and asked as to how many accidents the car had been in. The body damage was something that could not be hidden or denied. The entire passenger side as well as the passenger side corners of the bumpers were in very bad shape. It looked as though the car had slide sideways into an object on more than one occasion.

I let the son know that the car was a wholesale piece and that there was no way the car was worth even close to the $12k he was looking for. My managers put $1,500.00 on the car and given the reality check my customers got, they were quite happy with that and were even more happy that I was up front with them about their trade. End of story...they went home with a brand new Sentra.

Getting Real and Being Realistic

As much as you may think that the 6 cylinder car of yours that is currently running on 5 and has some pretty serious dents in the doors is not worth the value you think it is. Suck it up. Even though you want to be able to maximize your trade value, sometimes it just cannot be possible.

Another instance of this is with aftermarkets. While you may have dropped a bundle on your vehicle for a lift kit, cold air intake, have tuned the engine, and made other modifications, you have basically wasted money. The truth is that before you even considering trading that vehicle take all that stuff off and have the original parts put back on. Those modifications generally will not pass state inspection and the cost to replace those parts can be costly to you on your value. Just because you spent the money for those mods does not mean that it was worth it.

When you buy a vehicle, you just don't buy it for the next couple of years. You buy it for the many years down the road. Plan ahead now and think before you jump into modifying your car. Unless it is going to be a show piece you intend to have until the day you die, don't do any major upgrades that wouldn't pass a state inspection.

Chapter 7 – Knowing When To Buy

You've seen them, the countless ads on TV promoting one sale after another. It can be extremely confusing as a consumer to determine when it is the right time to buy a car. But it's this confusion that the dealers are counting on. Just because a sale looks amazing doesn't really mean that it is. What this means for you is that you need to be wary if what you are looking for is that brand new car.

No matter how you break it down, there will always be times that it will be better to buy that pickup truck than others. The same goes for sedans and coupes. It is in understanding this sales cycle that will help you save money. Just as in couponing, even the auto industry has its cycles.

Looking for that incredible **sedan**? No problem. The best incentives can be found around major holidays such as Memorial Day, President's Day, or end of model year sell down. In between these times, if you can't wait for a holiday or after the new models roll out, look for vehicles that have been on the lot the longest. Since dealerships have a couple of month's leeway on new inventory before they start getting hit with fees from the manufacturer, buyers can capitalize on buying older inventory. These savings can amount to as much as a couple of thousand dollars.

Depending on where you live, **pickup trucks** have an "off season" for the most part. It is interesting to see the lots change over time when during the spring, and summer, more trucks get traded in while in the late fall, you'll find it more difficult to locate that perfect 4 wheel drive truck.

One of the best times to nab a truck is during the off season when manufacturers may add more incentives to increase sales on those vehicles. As with sedans, keep an eye out for the oldest stock. The longer it has been there, the better it will be priced. The same holds true for the full-sized SUVs.

Coupes/sports cars are an interesting vehicle in and of themselves and have a similar sales cycle than trucks, though exactly the opposite. Coupes more often than not get traded in the late fall on into winter, while springtime brings the sports car enthusiast out of hiding and on to the lots.

The ideal time to buy a coupe is during the warm weather holidays when the sales are at their peak or just before the cold weather hits. Granted, the majority of sports cars and coupes out there are rear wheel drive vehicles and don't do well in the snow, so be sure to determine early on in your research whether or not that hot little 8 cylinder coupe is going to be the right fit.

Crossovers have their own special category. Since they combine the best of both a sedan and SUV, there is no particular sales cycle. As with the sedans, the best times to buy are during the major sales and old age units that may have been overlooked for a few months.

Whenever you are in question as to how long a vehicle has been on the lot, simply go to the dealer's website. Most dealerships today list two prices on their vehicles, as mentioned earlier. The trick is to find two vehicles of the same model that have very nearly the same MSRP. Then you will look at the sale price. The vehicle that has the biggest discount is the one that has been there the longest. If you're daring enough, wait an additional month if you can, particularly if it is off season for that unit. By waiting until the next calendar month, you may be able to score an even bigger discount.

Coupons
Believe it or not, dealerships have begun offering coupons that you can print at home

and bring in with you. Typically these coupons are only valid for the month or the timeframe that the dealership is promoting, but if combined with the right rebates, dealer incentives, and unit, it could amount to as much as an additional $500 off of your purchase. The key here is timing to help create that perfect storm of savings for you.

When I talk about timing, I mean after the price has been nailed down and you are happy with it. That is when you will whip out your coupon. HOWEVER…IF YOU ARE ASKED BEFOREHAND IF THERE ARE ANY OTHER DISCOUNTS YOU MAY QUALIFY FOR, DO NOT LIE AND TRY TO SNEAK IT IN AT THE END. At no time is it ever ok for you to lie in order to get a good deal, and that is not something I condone, nor do I suggest you do it.

Rewards Points

If you are doing business with a dealership you have bought from in the past and have gotten your service done there, be sure to have the sales manager check your rewards points balance. Since many dealerships have a rewards program for loyalty, you will want to see what all those points will amount to in terms of additional money off. Some dealerships will translate those points into as much as $1500 off of your vehicle purchase. Bear in mind, it can take several years to accumulate those kinds of points, so remember this when you are deciding on your initial purchase.

Likewise, if you are having a good experience with the dealership and believe you may purchase from them, be sure to ask about a rewards program. This can help you out in the future should you choose to do business with them again.

Not all dealerships offer rewards programs, and this should not be a deciding factor in where you make your purchase. The biggest factor you will want to take into consideration is how they price their vehicles. If they are completely transparent, then it is all systems go.

Freebies
Not all freebies are free. It's important to be careful of the freebies a dealership promises. There are usually hidden terms and conditions associated with them that could easily nullify the free services.

One such term could be in the case of free oil changes. Be sure to find out before you sign on the line as to what the terms are. More often than not, there is a mileage "clause" that, if you are not aware of it, could end up causing you to lose out on the free service.

The same holds true for "engine for life" guarantees. Should you fail to have the dealership perform one routine service that is recommended by the manufacturer, then this valuable service is just as useless as the paper it was printed on.

On the surface, some of the free programs may look incredible. Beware! Not all programs are transparent and certainly not all dealerships are honest and up front with their programs. Do your homework before you commit to the purchase.

Chapter 8 – Looking At The Additional Services

Understanding what the additional services or products are can help you to make an informed and intelligent decision. While some of them are not necessary, there are some that can be worthwhile and definitely useful. I'm going to be breaking down each one individually and explaining them and give my opinion. I'm also going to tell you how you can save money with these services.

Undercoating

This is an interesting concept. Most cars manufactured today already have a coating applied to the underside of the vehicle. This is especially true for vehicles that are shipped overseas since they MUST be protected from the salt air which can cause corrosion.

The best thing to do is to look at the Monroni sticker (commonly referred to as the window sticker) and see if there is an undercoating listed on the far left side. The left of the window sticker lists all of the items the vehicle has as a base model. Sometimes you can find that the vehicle has already had an undercoating applied right at factory level. When in doubt, bring someone who knows what to look for and look under the vehicle.

If the vehicle DOES NOT have a protective undercoating and you live in a region where salt on the roads is a daily sight, decide for yourself as to whether or not you want this. Not only can it extend the structural life of the vehicle, but it may in some instances help give the vehicle equity a boost down the road.

Be sure to negotiate on this. What the dealership sells it for is not the bottom line price and there is definitely a profit margin here.

Gap Insurance
The first few years you have a vehicle financed, there is a definite fiscal imbalance between the value of the vehicle and what is owed on the loan. And it never seems to fail that a car that has just been purchased seems to have a big bull's-eye on it and every chucklehead on the road manages to come straight at you.

Here's how gap insurance works. Let's say you bought a car 6 months ago for $20,000.00. You financed a total of $23,500.00 at 3.99% interest. You get into a major accident and the insurance company totals your car. They value your car at $18,000.00 at the time of your accident and the loan payoff at that time is $26,500.00. The insurance company will pay the bank the VALUE of the vehicle, which leaves you in a deficiency. This means that you still owe the bank $7,500.00. That's a big ouch, especially if you absolutely must have a vehicle for work.

Gap insurance is what comes to the rescue. As long as you have the plan, that is. With a deficient balance due on a totaled vehicle, gap insurance swoops in and pays that difference meaning you can walk away from the loan knowing that it will not negatively impact your credit and will be paid off completely.

There are only two instances where I do not recommend getting gap, and unless you are in one of these two categories, get it.

The first is in the event of a down payment of at least 35%. This kind of down payment will negate any negative equity situation that could come back and bite you in the butt later as long as you qualify for a prime interest rate.

The second is if you are paying for the entire vehicle in cash. With cash deals, gap insurance is irrelevant and unnecessary. However, if you are one of those that will be financing the brunt of the purchase, get the gap, but be sure to negotiate the price. This is another service that has a profit margin, so don't be afraid to go for the discount, especially where being payment conscious is concerned.

Service Contracts

Service contracts are another item that can be negotiated. The cost of these varies between packages and the particular model of the car, the age, and the mileage can all impact the final price of it. The most expensive one I have seen to date was on a used vehicle with moderate mileage and was the platinum package (meaning the only things not covered were normal wear and tear items).

These service contracts can be very helpful…and save you lots of money in the long run. While most people out there will say you don't need it because of the manufacturer's warranty, remember that the warranty typically only covers defects in the parts used to build your vehicle, and do not cover breakdowns of particular parts from normal use.

Take the fuel pump for example. Your brand-new Malibu that only has 12,000 miles on it and it suffers fuel pump failure. This could be considered defective. However, let's say that your car is 4 years old and has 50,000 miles on it. While some manufacturers' warranties will have already expired, others may not have. Still, the vehicle being the age it is with the mileage it has will generally not have the fuel pump covered. This leaves you footing the bill for what can be an expensive repair.

Service contracts generally work on the same principal as medical insurance. You will most likely have a co-pay when you take your vehicle in for the repairs.

Another reason to opt for the vehicle service contract is quite simple and should be obvious...the unknown. When it comes to pre-owned vehicles, you don't know what the driving habits were of the person or persons who owned the car before you. If a particular vehicle has had more than one owner, the chances of there being issues with the vehicle are increased.

I am always amazed at the number of "experts" out there that say you don't need a service contract when there is a manufacturer warranty still in place. What these people don't realize is that there are a very large number of exclusions that come with that. One of them has to do with the vehicle maintenance. If a prior owner did not maintain the vehicle as required by the manufacturer, and a problem arises after you have made the purchase, they are not liable for the repair costs and generally will not pay for any damages as a result. This is why I always say that while it may cost a little more up front it is better to be safe than sorry.

Service Packages

Some dealerships will offer you a service package. These packages often will offer free oil changes, loaner cars, multi-point inspections, and other services for a fee. It is vitally important for you to weigh out the cost with and without it before you make a final decision. Granted, these packages can save you couple of thousand dollars, but those savings are generally diminished on cars that only require oil changes every 6 months or less. Do the math yourself before you commit to a package that may or may not benefit you.

Chapter 9 – Finalizing The Deal

Now that you have decided on a car, have gotten the approval, and agree to the terms, it's time to head into the finance office. This is where people tend to get more nervous than before. RELAX! The hard part is done.

Dealing With The Paperwork

The finance manager that is working with you should break everything down for you and basically recap all that you have agreed to up to this point. This is also the point where you will negotiate the cost on the extra services that you would like.

As he or she goes through each document with you, be sure they explain everything thoroughly. Do not sign a single document unless they have answered any and all questions you have about anything that is on that document. If you need them to slow down a bit because they are going faster than what is comfortable for you, then speak up. Don't be afraid to take all of the time you need to mentally process all of the information that is on those documents. They are legally binding and that means it is all on you if you just go ahead and sign, then realize a week later you didn't fully comprehend what was there in black and white.

Finance managers as a whole are not bad people. While there are some out there that are shady and will try to slip something past you, the vast majority are aboveboard and will do what they can to accommodate you.

Here are a couple of things to remember about your experience in the finance office....

1. All additional services will be offered to you <u>before</u> the purchase order is printed and signed. If you are feeling pressured to buy a service you don't want, be assertive and hold your ground. Only take the add-ons that you know will benefit you. If they try to force you to take something you don't want, get up and start to walk out without saying a word. Guaranteed they will change their tune very quickly.

2. You have the right as the buyer to fully understand all the terms and

conditions of the contract. After you have gone through all of the terms and covered the lender that has approved you and the interest rate, if there is any variance to anything prior to going into the finance office (aside from the add-ons which probably have not been figured in yet), question it.

The Reviews Speak for Themselves

When you were first doing your research on the dealership, your investigations should have included what others have said about that dealership and the reputation that it has. This is a huge thing. Granted, the average person will be more likely to post a negative comment rather than a positive one, so take the number of negatives with a grain of salt. It is the content of the comments that should concern you the most and it is those that a picture of the overall dealings will emerge.

If a number of people all posted similar experiences in the finance department then you can bet that you will probably have an issue as well. This is particularly true if the comments are fairly recent and close together in timeframe. It is imperative that when it comes to the financing department that you not be afraid to grow a backbone and learn how to use it. This is especially true if people you know tell you that you are too nice, don't know how to say no, or tend to be a doormat for people.

Now, this is not to say that the finance manager is going to try and take you for everything you got. They aren't. They have a goal to accomplish and that is to sell the add-on products as well as finalize all of the paperwork. Some of the add-ons can save you thousands over the course of ownership. Some won't. For the most part, it is going to depend greatly on whether or not you're paying 50% or greater with cash.

Your total time in the finance office should not exceed 45 minutes, unless you choose to read every single word of every single document put in front of you.

Once you are finished up in the finance office, if it hasn't happened already, your salesperson will put the license plate (or temp tag) on your new vehicle and you can transfer all of your belongings. CONGRATULATIONS! You have made it to the finish line and as long as you followed all of my advice, the next few years of payments should breeze by and you will be able to save some money. If you pay a little extra with each payment, then you should be able to shorten your term greatly.

Chapter 10 – Buying A Car With Derogatory (Bad) Credit

Things go wrong in life and sometimes you get a financial smack down that leaves your credit in a shambles. This can leave you in a bad spot, especially when buying a car. There are some very basic, but honest, truths you need to deal with before you go out car shopping.

Regardless of whether or not you want to believe it, but when you have a challenged credit score, you need to me even more diligent about your purchase and how to go about it.

Here are 14 truths you need to understand completely before you head to a dealership to buy the car of your dreams. These truths will hold true anywhere in the country.

Truth #1 – As much as you want to buy that $40,000.00 car with no money down, the reality is that it will not happen. With bad credit, the goal is to rebuild and show the lenders that you can manage your money effectively and responsibly. This can be a tall task when you're recovering from a financial meltdown.

In reality, you will generally qualify for a car loan up to $20,000.00, depending on your credit score and condition of your credit profile. There are other things that will also need to be in place in order to secure that approval.

Truth #2 – You are going to need to have money down. End of story, and there's no getting around it. The main point is for there to be positive equity in the vehicle that you are buying. Truth be told, you will need to have more money down on a used car than you will a new one. This is because on a new car, the equity is generally equal to the MSRP. On a used car, the equitable amount is the bookout value, which is generally less than the retail value. This bookout value is also referred to as the loan value. It is fair to say that on a new car, you will want to put down at the very least taxes, tags, and fees.

In reality, it is far easier to get someone with bad credit into a new vehicle than a used. And when it comes to down payment, your best option is to put down 10-25% of the purchase price of the vehicle, depending on how low your credit score is. This will make you look more desirable to banks and increase your chances of getting the loan. Bear in mind, the lower your credit score, the higher the down payment you will need to have in order to get financed without a qualified co-buyer.

Truth #3 – If you recently changed jobs, you are going to need to show at least 2 years of work history on your credit application. If you have had more than two jobs in that two year period, then you are in a pickle.

The same goes for your residence. If you often make like a grasshopper and jump from address to address, you are only hurting yourself. The banks want to see stability, and this is demonstrated in your length of employment and residency.

Truth #4 – If you think the answer to your transportation woes lay in the form of a buy-here-pay-here car lot, guess again. The sad reality is that you can easily end up paying at least 4 times what the vehicle is truly worth. Furthermore, these car often have accidents on the Carfax history, have high mileage, and typically have mechanical issues. This means that the car is really worth next to nothing. This is not to say that all cars purchased at a buy-here-pay-here lot are bad. Once in a while you can find a good one, but they are few and far between.

Sadly, many people with bad credit flock to these lots in order to get the low payment. When you do the math, the payment really isn't all that low for what you're getting. They are typically a weekly payment, and when you figure out your monthly cost, it can easily be $300 a month or more, depending on the vehicle. You still need to have about $1500 to $2500 down, and that being the case, it is far more worth it to put down that money on a vehicle that will have a better trade value 3-5 years down the road. In a nutshell....steer clear of the buy-here-pay-here lots. Not only will you end up with a car that will have a very low value in less than 2 years, but you will be doing nothing to rebuild your credit since these car lots generally do not report to the credit bureaus.

Truth #5 – When it comes to interest rate, the unfortunate news is that you will without a doubt have a higher interest rate. There is no way around that. There are a few factors that will affect your interest rate:

- ❖ Amount financed
- ❖ Credit score
- ❖ Overall credit profile
- ❖ Down payment (certain lenders)
- ❖ Overall stability

While interest rate is generally preconceived from all of the ads you see on television, the tough pill to swallow is that you will not qualify for the prime interest rates with a low credit score. It is also the interest rate that will be the final factor in determining your monthly payment, so if you have it in your head that you want a $200 a month payment on an $18,000.00 car, you better start counting up how much you have to put down because it just is not going to happen.

Remember the rule of thumb....for every $1,000 financed, you can generally count on about $20 a month in payment. The variable in this is a poor credit score of 525 or lower, in which case you can figure on about $25 a month for every $1,000 financed. Keep in mind....THIS IS JUST A GUIDE. This formula is meant to help you in setting your purchase and payment goals.

Truth #6 – Buying a cheap car privately to avoid the hassle of the traditional car loan can cost you a fortune. Since private sellers are required by law in most states that they only need to provide a clear car title, this can leave you in a serious bind. Most states have inspection laws which may or may not include emissions inspections. A private seller is not required to sell you a vehicle that will pass inspection. They are only required to divulge the issues they are aware of.

The short story about this is that you can find a great deal on a car, but find out the hard way that it will end up costing you more than a couple of thousand dollars for it to be able to pass inspection. Further on down the line you can experience further problems. This doesn't even cover the issue of an accident that the owner conveniently doesn't tell you about. Regardless, the Carfax generally tells all...for the most part.

The easiest way to avoid being taken, or ending up with even more financial difficulty is to avoid the private seller completely. This is not to say that all private sellers are horrible people looking to scam the first person that comes along. They aren't. It simply means that the majority of private sellers have no clue that the thump they hear when they make a turn could be something serious and are not licensed mechanics.

Truth #7 – Bankruptcy is not the kiss of death to your credit. As long as your bankruptcy has been discharged and you haven't fallen into the same pitfalls, you should be fine. Again, it is imperative that you have a good chunk of money down. The banks will see the bankruptcy on your credit profile and it tends to make them nervous. The more money you put down, in their eyes, it makes you look that much more serious about buying a car and keeping up with your payments.

Truth #8 – Even with bad credit or no credit, it is entirely possible to save money on your car purchase. This is easily accomplished in two ways:

A) The larger the down payment, the less you will be financing and you will have less money dished out over the term of the loan in interest. The higher the principle you lay out in the beginning, the fatter your wallet will be in the end.

B) Since you know you will have a higher interest rate and much more spent in total interest charges, you need to shorten the term of the loan. If you take the 72 month term, fine. BUT, each month, pay additional and direct it towards the principle of the loan. This will do two things; your car will be paid off sooner, and you will be paying less in interest. Keep in mind that there are some second chance lenders out there that have a fixed interest schedule which means that early payoff will not reduce the amount of interest paid. Be sure to ask your finance manager, and if they are not sure, have him call the bank directly to find out.

Despite these common things, provided you make your payments on time consistently, you will have no trouble being able to handle the next truth.

Truth #9 – Just because you bought it, doesn't mean you're married to it. What this means to you is that there is no rule that says you have to stay in that vehicle for the full term of the loan. You have the option of trading during the loan term (though you WILL have negative equity, so be careful in this) or you can pay additional each month so that you can pay off the loan early. There are no penalties for early payoff, so use this to your advantage.

Truth #10 – The chances of you being able to pick and choose the car of your dreams and get approved on it are slim to none if you don't have a huge amount of cash to put down. What I mean by this is that if you're looking at a full-size pickup truck or a large sedan, you had better be able to put down 50% of the vehicle price. Otherwise, to increase your chances of being able to get financed at all, when you go to the dealership, there is one question you must ask the salesperson...."I have bad credit. What vehicles will be the best options for me?"

There is no shame in being straightforward about your credit situation. As a salesperson, I have always appreciated that kind of honesty and it makes me want to go out of my way even more to help the person get into a vehicle.

Truth #11 – Trading a vehicle in on a new model is a great thing, as long as you don't have a ton of negative equity. Negative equity is the difference between what the vehicle is worth and what is owed on the loan when the payoff amount is greater than the value. For example: Your car may be worth $5,000.00, but the payoff amount is $10,000.00. This means that you have $5,000.00 of negative equity to roll into the new loan.

This is a tricky situation and can ultimately result in you being declined for the loan. The only way around this is to come up with a large amount of cash to put down. This down payment is dependent on how low your credit score is, but in order to protect the credit score, you can figure on having to put down the amount of the negative equity plus an additional 10-25% of the vehicle purchase price.

While I am on this topic….math is math. It is simple and absolute. In this I mean that you cannot roll negative equity into a new loan with minimal down payment and expect a lower monthly payment. It cannot and will not happen, so if this is your goal…use the formula I gave you earlier to make your comparison and be realistic about what you can afford to purchase. The only difference in the formula is that you will need to figure on adding in what you figure your negative equity will be if you already know roughly what your car is worth and what the payoff amount is.

Truth #12 – Going from dealership to dealership trying to a buy a car with the terms of no more than $500 down and a prime interest rate is not only defeatist, it is going to sink your already damaged credit score even further down the tubes. If you managed to get an approval with a 525 credit score at 18% interest with $1500 down, having your credit pulled all over God's creation will only cause the banks to require you to put down even more money, end up with a higher interest rate than what you were initially approved on and see your credit score drop from dealership to dealership. There is a reason for this, and it's one you need to pay attention to.

Regardless of what your credit score is, each time your credit gets pulled, it creates an inquiry. Each inquiry costs you 2 points of your credit score. These inquiries will stay on your credit bureau for 2 years. Not only that, but each bank and dealership that pulls your credit can see as to where you have been shopping and which banks have looked at your credit.

It never ceases to amaze me as to how some people come in with derogatory credit and know it is in that state, and still walk in with all the arrogance they can muster and get angry because they couldn't get a prime rate. This brings me to my next truth......

Truth #13 – There are two types of people out there with derogatory credit: those who got smacked by bad luck and a crappy economy, and those that habitually open lines of credit, especially cell phones and credit cards, and don't pay on them intentionally.

The first group I genuinely feel for…life has batted them upside the head and sent them into a financial tailspin that can sometimes lead to bankruptcy.

The second group, however, they have earned their credit score and that is not a compliment. What you don't realize is that while banks and the sales managers at the dealerships can see your credit score, they can also see every single account that has hit your credit bureau for the past 7 years. This includes payment history, current account status, collections accounts, repossessions, foreclosures, bankruptcies, medical bills, and judgments. It is abundantly apparent to the banks (as well as anyone who is privy to this information) as to which type of person the banks are dealing with….the first type or the second.

While I am on the topic of bouncing from dealership to dealership, not only are you killing your credit score but you are wasting your time (which as I said earlier in the book has a dollar value) and wasting your money. As hard of a pill as it is to swallow, don't be afraid to just grab the bull by the horns and get it done. You have to start somewhere, and one cannot start in the middle.

True Story – *A woman came into the dealership one day needing a vehicle. Her car was totaled in an accident and she was in a rental courtesy of the insurance company. She was quite open with me and stated that her credit score was 618.*

While her credit score was low, it wasn't hateful and she could easily buy a new but inexpensive vehicle with a $1,000.00 down.

After we picked out a car that fit all of her needs, we ran her credit. Wonder among wonders her credit score came up 120 points BELOW where she said it was just a couple of days prior. Looking at her bureau, the cause was apparent and I became direct.

Over the course of the previous two days, she had been bouncing from dealership to dealership, having her credit run and submitted at each one. There were more than 55 inquiries on her profile and that said it all. When I asked her as to why she did that, she simply said that it was because she didn't like the interest rate she had been given.

After 45 minutes of explaining to her the reason why she couldn't buy a car that day, let alone get a prime interest rate, she left rather upset. Whether or not she believed me is irrelevant. The big issue here is she damned herself with all of the inquiries and being naïve enough to think that she could get a prime interest rate just because she wanted it.

Truth #14 – Getting an auto loan with derogatory credit is not as cut and dry as you might think. The chances are very high that the bank will require you to provide documents proving your income, residency, bank account status, discharge of bankruptcy, etc. If you claim that you make $600 a week at a job that you claim you have been working at for 6 months, you had better be able to prove $2400 a month in income for all six of those months. Let's say you claimed the above, but your year-to-date income only shows $4500 and one of your paystubs shows a gross pay of $2300....now you have a problem. While your income is more than sufficient, when the bank does the math to make sure it all adds up, and you come up short.

My next point is this....even though the bank is asking for documents to verify everything, if you can prove it, suck it up and put them together. Don't bounce from dealership to dealership just because you don't want to have to do the work to finalize the loan and get on your way with a vehicle. What the banks require is not going to change, and in fact, refer back to Truth # 13 regarding bouncing from dealership to dealership.

Yes, it can be a pain in the butt, but in order to get past the conditional approval and into a vehicle what has YOUR name on the title, you will just have to grin and bear it. You have to start somewhere, so you might as well make it easier on yourself instead of running around trying to find that prime approval that will elude you until you rebuild your credit score back up into the 700's.

To Sum It All Up

These truths are just that....they are the truth. And while they are the truth, understand that on occasion there is the slight variation based on other variables we have covered in this book, such as credit profile.

When it comes to trying to rebuild your credit, or even if you have started out with absolutely no credit at all, the best advice can only come from a credit counselor, just as a credit counselor isn't going to try and tutor you in all things couponing, or the art of car shopping.

Everything that has been contained in these pages is the culmination of my expertise and education that I have received in the sales arena over the course of the past 23 years. While the processes have changed, the principles have not. It is your credit score that speaks for you, and while I have met some completely terrific people that desperately needed my help.

The biggest thing that you need to understand is that regardless of your credit score, it is entirely possible to purchase a car and not go broke doing it. Follow all of my advice and you will do very well.

And while we are talking about how you will end up making out...when things get tight, or even before they have a chance to get that way, search out my other book, "Mrs. Tightwad's Guide to Couponing" and learn what it means to have saved extra money each month from groceries to put towards your down payment, a vacation, an addition on your home, or whatever you want. Just remember to keep the pantry (and the gas tank) full and keep it cheap!

~Mrs. Tightwad